STORIES SHE TELLS

STORIES SHE TELLS

Poems by

HADINET TEKIE

Stories She Tells
Published by Hadinet Tekie

Copyright ©2022 Hadinet Tekie.

All rights reserved.

No part of this book may be reproduced in any form or by any mechanical means, including information storage and retrieval system without permission in writing from the publisher/author, except by a reviewer who may quote passages in a review.

All images, logos, quotes, and trademarks included in this book are subject to use according to trademark and copyright laws of the United Kingdom.

TEKIE, HADINET, Author
STORIES SHE TELLS
HADINET TEKIE

ISBNs
Paperback: 978-1-80227-536-0
eBook: 978-1-80227-537-7
Hardback: 978-1-80227-538-4

All rights reserved by Hadinet Tekie.
www.dekove.me

I dedicate this collection to my beautiful mother,
Leghesa Mascio,
who taught me strength and perseverance daily,
through actions rather than words.
I love you, Mum.

THANK YOU

I see you
Like I see shadows and lights
Intricately you weave
In winds and beats

I hear you
Through heart and soul
Softly you whisper to me
I'm here
I'm you

I feel you
As I feel my hand
My pulse
My flesh

I come to be where you end
End where you begin

I hold you
Infinitely near
Through tears and laughs
Memories and goals

All I am thanks you
My mum
For choosing me
Your daughter

Rest in peace, Mum
1960–2022

CONTENTS

ARDOR — 1

LEAPS AND FALLS	3
TRAILS OF US	4
NEVER GONE	5
BEWITCHED	6
LABYRINTH	8
THE TRUTH	9
WHAT IF	10
HARD KISS	11
SCARLET HAZE	12
RITORNA	13
I OFFER YOU	14
GONE	15
SONGS AND RHYMES	16
SPELLBOUND	17
VIRTUAL LOVE	18
INGRAINED	19
WET KISS	20
REGINA	21
DEAR SISTER	22
REMAINS	23

DEAD OF NIGHT	24
SCORCHED	25
BETWEEN THE LIPS	26
BLUE BLACK	27
FIRES AND LIGHTS	28

INJURIA — 29

THICK LOVE	31
INJUSTICIA	32
TRUTH OR DARE	33
BLEED THROUGH	34
THE UNCONSCIOUS HURT	35
PREDATOR OR PREY	36
RED SNOW	37
GASP	38
DEAD ALIVE	39
OBLIVION	40
SOFT KILL 2.0	41
APOLOGY NOT ACCEPTED	42
THAT I AM WOMAN	43
RED PHOENIX	44
CONFRONTATION	45
REAPER	46
ARMOURED	47
CHOCKER	48
ROOTS	49

HIDDEN SMILE	50
SILENT SABOTAGE	51
SECRETS	52
INVASION	53
CLAWS	55
BEHIND CLOSED DOORS	56

VITA — 59

KRONOS	61
BURNT	62
THE STRUGGLE	63
UNDERWATER	64
ENCHANTING NIGHT	65
BETWEEN RIGHT AND WRONG	66
FUNHOUSE	67
NEW DAY	68
INSOMNIA	69
THE GLINT IN YOUR EYE	70
HANTU AIR	71
LIKE CRYSTALS	72
STORIES SHE TELLS	73
MORNING AFTER	74
EARTHLY SPLENDOR	75
ALWAYS RIGHT	76
FIGHTER	77
BLUE GRASS	78

REBORN	79
SHIFTER	80
GAZE LIKE MINE	81
UNTRUTHS	82
FEATHERS	83
DEAD ASLEEP	84
ZEST OF HOPE	85
ABOUT THE AUTHOR	87
CREDITS	88

*"We are so accustomed to disguise ourselves to others,
that in the end, we become disguised to ourselves."*

François de La Rochefoucauld

ARDOR

LEAPS AND FALLS

Challenged faith leaps from colourless abyss
Hopes of fuchsia dreams mingle in golden streaks of honest
   rays
Constant pourings of heart and soul arise

You mingle

Aimlessly you drift in silent ripples of dusted love

You save me from myself

Unable to foresee the truth beyond
I blindly leap into the unknown
And gladly fall into my hope

TRAILS OF US

Bleeding fires in fleeting clouds
Drip ash of love and hate alike
Through waxen wants they spread
Loving completely
Hating utterly
Longing thoroughly
Flames reach past limits
Freely they wander
Leaving trails of you and I behind

NEVER GONE

You are everywhere
I feel your essence
In all I see
and
Touch
Memories remain
Made flesh by love

BEWITCHED

Flesh and blood play out like lightning
Villain's touch takes a willing heart pronouncing a death sentence
Sounds of night awaken me
Whilst flames of gossip engulf
Take me to a new level

I am exposed

A wandering savage searching for something unknown
I hunt for myself
My soul
He holds my heart in a death-like grip
Unwilling to let go
Chained
Imprisoned
Forever his
His presence surrounds
Reminds me of what I cannot forget
Cruelly he rips
Slowly I die
A hounded slave
Hell and despair are upon me
I refuse to awaken at any touch but his

In him I wrap a thousand onward years
While the drops I distil shall grow fierce
Possessive

Of him I love day and night
Fulfilled
United with myself
Do you exist?
Or are you just a figment?
Painful reality scares me
Yet I am drawn
Like a moth to a flickering flame
Breaking through barriers of time
My destiny
Be with me always

LABYRINTH

Maze like trails lead to you
Enveloped in flares of history
They fuse and conceal
Every step a lure
Enticing me closer
Reverberating visions of adventures
Fantastically they unwind
Blurred steps made of melody
Lose me in a star filled world
Magically pulled down gems
Wrap around in silken gloom
Drape over scattered memories
Close of eyes and I see you
Beguiling me on

THE TRUTH

Like a never ending river flowing to its source

I want more
I want love
I want happiness
I want passion
I want respect
I won't settle for less
I won't settle for you

WHAT IF

What if I fill my heart with you?
Will I still feel nothing?

What if I feel my thoughts of you?
Will they mesh into oblivion?

What if time stood still?
Would it change the future?

What if I give up on you?
Will I be giving up on myself?

HARD KISS

I kiss you dry
My oasis
My want
My need
I love you hard
Thick as tar
Deep as the earth's core
My balance
My centre
My heart

SCARLET HAZE

I slather
A thick layer of scarlet fever
Between love petals
of rose

Heated beat
Trips
Slowly
Into the next
Rhythmically
They lull

Sleep
Becomes
You

In all its fevered simplicity
Hypnotic in your rise
and fall
You ripple
and ebb away

An echo of silence remains

RITORNA

Waxed memory
Infused deep within
Waxed portal
Transports me to you
Like magic
Created from nothing
Moulded and shaped
It breathes back life
It breathes back you

I OFFER YOU

I offer deep wine
The type that spreads itself through you in one gulp
That mixes blindly with your blood
Warming you and all around

I offer you distressed sunsets
Filled with fulfilled desires and aching cravings
Framed by forever changing skies

I offer you clear moons
Stroked by silver and magic
Carrying sultry memories and nostalgia

I offer you the sweetest sounds and fluid motions of youth
Cradled by sentimental notes
Of times gone and those to be

GONE

At night stillness takes me
I sit drifting into nothing
My limbs heavy with air
My heart light to the touch
It beats
It carries you within
In folds and stars

SONGS AND RHYMES

I know you
Like my own hand

Your thoughts are mine
They speak to me
They tell me your story

Through songs and rhymes
Linked by a certainty of what was
What is
What will be

Like musical notes I float
Inch by inch
Invisible step
by
Invisible step

I reach out
Ever softly
Pluck your heart
Ever softly
You pluck mine

You knew me
Like your own hand

SPELLBOUND

Whisper to me
Web a dream
Coloured tightly in abstract care
Starry prediction
Painted in oily hope
Accurate
In its shiny end
Fan my wings
With spider web of lies
Reach the skies
Brushing fiery stars alight
Polish me up while looking down
Into dark and light
I drown

VIRTUAL LOVE

What would you do if our lives were threaded into one?
I know
It's easy to link and disconnect
A click
A breath
A sigh
A temporary soulmate
A pending connection
A ghosted love haunts
Virtually looking
Hoping
Doubting
Fairy-tale endings
Hello?
Hi?
Are you there?
I have something important to say . . .
100 coins to read the message

INGRAINED

Shave off my skin

Layer by layer

Slivers of rainbow trapped in light

Flecked in want

Bleed out golden hue

Seep in love and hate

Catch me in velvet

Wrap me in lust

Forever yours

Forever mine

WET KISS

Warm rain kisses me wet
I breathe
Sky high
Eyes close
Lips tingle drops
Skin opens
I stand
Still
Being kissed

REGINA

Cut me quick
To my marrow
Scoop me whole
On your lap
Patch me swiftly
With love and care
Carry me deeply
In your heart

DEAR SISTER

Fingers stroke
Thirsting warmth
Seeking solace
Each stroke
A silent cry
A lament heard by none but me
Digging my core
Scraping my being
Scooping me out
Thumbnail stabs an imprint
A crescent stamp
"Once I was here"
Don't forget me little sis

REMAINS

Arched into obscurity
You cradle my world
Steeped in time
You settle yourself

Breathe in you
Breathe out me

Dark in your corners
You stay hidden
entwined
In a past
Of us

A universe of rewinds awaits within
Enveloping all our hazed wants
Swallowing all our needs

Incessantly you hunger
Repeatedly you take
A husk of me remains

Breathe in you
Breathe out you

DEAD OF NIGHT

I'd take you
My sole light

When all sleep
I'd pluck stars for you

I'd cheat and raid
Rob velvets and silks
Cunning hands would seize
Grasping while searching
You'd hide between your blacks
Never unfolding
Ally or foe

To me you are the night

SCORCHED

Hard pit
Made of heart
Softly slides into its crease

It lies

Wrinkling me whole
Leaving no trace of order
Leaving no trace of us

BETWEEN THE LIPS

I empty the glass dry
Each gulp covers
Parched
Dry lips
Reaches and expands
Returns what once was
Lights its path
All is seen
Nothing missed
It glides through crevices and secrets
Touches the untouched
Strokes the truths and lies
Tasting their promise

BLUE BLACK

Into the blue it blackens
I see blind
I hear by wet touch
I endure by fate

Into the blue it freezes
It speaks of times past
It speaks of you
It speaks of silence

FIRES AND LIGHTS

Glitter flickers in dim horizon
Shimmering all that covers
You stand outlined by shine
Hollow in core and mind
Encircled by light that does not touch
I feel my pain in you forever more
Hug last of my light to you
Like a firefly you leave a trail
Of
What is
What could be
And
What will be

THICK LOVE

I want to make it so that any woman that looks at you will
    turn to stone by the hundreds of snakes that'll hiss my
    name to her
I want it so that when you run, dance or go to the sauna
    you'll sweat me all over you
Drip my name deep into your pores
I want my senses to envelop yours

You will not see me coming but you'll not want me to go

Your breath will connect to mine
Solid in its need and want

My heart will be safe in yours
Like a vault with me as your combination

INJUSTICIA

I know you
I know why you are you
Danger is inevitable
One of us will die
Forgone conclusion
Pick a side
Slide in it
Shadows won't help you now
Shades of black uncovered
Say it
Once uttered it will never come back
It will spread and grow wings
Say it

Seal our fate

TRUTH OR DARE

Mine are dreams of yesteryears and days of hazy nights
Twinkling blue lies dipped in your truth
You slap my heart then kiss it better
I walk on a thin red line of possibilities
Free falling without a net of promises

I fall

Hard

Hard like silk raining down on me

BLEED THROUGH

Like rain I fall
Tangled in my own history
Rusty iron dusted into shades of past
Echoes filter lights and creviced blacks
Heavy in its velvet world
It crumples
Whole
Frozen at its last curtain call
Exit
Stage left

THE UNCONSCIOUS HURT

Passionate night is yours

Sinless whisper follows

Its hard on my soul

Without stars in my eyes

Cold

Dead to the touch

I glance behind where the losers despair

You hide between sorrows

No trick of the light

A drifter between worlds that glides into my life

Disrupter

Destroyer of routine

You see black while I see white

You promise the impossible and the gullible believes

Innocent tormenter

Unconsciously deceiving

Hurting

Torturing my soul

Crack my spirit

Slowly

In your own time

While my heart skips the beats and out of tune sings its own songs

PREDATOR OR PREY

Rows of meat alienate me from others
Hunter hunts its prey
Lay down the final card while wounded wounds and killers die
Darkness enfolds and hides
Light glimpses visions of tomorrows
Yesterdays submit relentlessly to another
Careless whisper prides itself
Agonies of hell burn deep in my soul
Roars of infidelity tear you apart
Claiming his last victim into oblivion

More arrive to take his place

RED SNOW

She runs
Towards danger
Not covered in signs
Fragrant out
Rotten in
No gleaming eyes or leering smile
No sharpened claws or pointed teeth

She runs
Safety unreached
Screams
Unable to tell if out
Or deep within
Mouth covered by evil
Not her body
Her gift not hers to give
Will she survive the first snow of the year?

GASP

I gasp for lungs
Filled with hope
Air thick with you
My helplessness complete
Clinging to this sad reality
My normality
Heart stomped
Years of footprints
Chalk outlines my past

Dirties my present

DEAD ALIVE

Slunched

I root

Here

Where I was reborn

Dead

A breathing husk

Wondering eyes

Reaching out

Grubby fingers grab

Dig deep

In the depths of nothing

Soiled

I sit

Fixed in place

Tied by love

Freed by hatred

Revived by wrath

OBLIVION

In the core of you and me
There is always the dead
In shadows of hate
It grows and spreads its wings
No place untouched or sacred
Latching on to running ankles
It pulls you back
Dragging howling hearts in shadows
They twist within themselves
Silence so loud it wakes my numb soul
Into oblivion
Living echoes of light and fire behind

SOFT KILL 2.0

Thick as old yoghurt
It penetrates your pores
Infuses itself like hope into your being
Golden green needle threads beneath your skin
Hits its target like a hammer's beat

APOLOGY NOT ACCEPTED

"Sorry"

"No"

"What do you mean no?"

"That's not what I want"

"I've apologized"

"I don't want your apology"

"What do you want?"

"I want you to hurt"

THAT I AM WOMAN

Woman dying giving life
Woman dying breathing her first
Woman bleeding monthly
Woman kissed black and blue by

Brother
Father
Husband
Son

Woman dressed for decoration
Human tinselled tree
Woman forced to smile while crying
Cradled pain
Cradled joy
Uncradled
Still she rises

Eyes that fight
Mouth that sets
Fists that fist

RED PHOENIX

In a cloudburst of red
I am enveloped
I lather in anguished foam
Soak in a blood bath of hate
Perfumed with scarlet sneers
I powder myself in ash
Gathered by my destruction
I am reborn
I will breathe fire and venom
Return the scars by a million shards of vengeance
Like a grim reaper I will reap
Leaving depraved specks of you behind

CONFRONTATION

Your anger angers me
Did you expect me to die too?
Socially as well as emotionally?
Did you think I was made of stone?
Stone breaks too
It crumbles
I bleed and cry slowly but painfully
You insult me with your words and looks
Put me down with your lack of trust

Tell me what you are thinking
What you want from me

Maybe I'll consent to stop my life with yours

REAPER

Tortured soul awaits sentence
Why appear disrupter
Executioner of love
In limbo
I linger
Hoping against odds
Why you and not him?
Life stands still while fates take over
Is he aware of his powers?
I scream out but he does not hear
I reach without promise

Will he ever?

ARMOURED

Putrid in my hate
Shrill in my war cry
I lunge in dark swarms
Eyes bright
Claws sharp
Death awaits those that steer
Bloodied tears drown thirsty earth
Cover hollowed ground
Trodden by many
Survived by none
I prepare for the coming
Remain armed with loathing and hate
Nothing left but sharpened grit
Glinting in the dark night
Fires twinkle like earth's stars
Dancing through acrid rain
Covering all with sultry glow

Concealing scarlet soul

CHOCKER

I choke on words
That crawl in me
Of hated letters
Of why I'm me

I choke on words
That won't come out
They lie silent
Dig in my mouth

I taste derision
It coats my tongue
A decay of struggles
Swallows me down

ROOTS

I come from your roots

Oceans of wants divide us

Forged through indifference

Blood thins like water

Transparently it trickles

and splashes

Leaving no evidence of its existence

Everything conditional

A badly scripted play

Lies tripping and coating themselves in sugar

Sour in my mouth

Covering my tongue in their acidity

I crave pure oxygen

To breathe true air in a desert filled with greedy sand

Time ticks slowly forward

Ticking the tocking at the pace of eternity

HIDDEN SMILE

I awaken to unseen reflection
Hollow in my marrow
Wounds and scars abound
Step by languid step
I layer me
Each stroke
A lie
A smile
A joke
Universally connected to
Each carved mask
Transparent in their daily act
I brush hair
Breathe in role
Breathe out being
Fear kisses me goodbye
While I step out into the unknown

SILENT SABOTAGE

Innocence is lost on you
Mocker of light
Your laugh ignites infernos
Spreads poison through ridicule
Vileness injected
Still
You laugh
Like a poisoned arrow
Take aim
Hit target

Leaving clones of you behind

SECRETS

I live in shades of me
Silently they lie

Surround me in a silky case

Unseen
Untouched
Unheard
I stay

I scream without a voice I hear

Rise high
Fan wings
With spider web of lies

Surround myself with wants and needs

Unseen
Untouched
Unheard

I cry

INVASION

High above I see you
Interested in your expected plea
You are sound in ways I cannot abide

I see your velvet thoughts as they glide past my own
Kill me with your stricken looks and vengeful gaze
Attacked I feel by your sordid mind
It soils my soul
It crowds me until I breathe not

Kisses of death handwritten by your lips as they brush upon
    mine
Softness deceitful with pain later bestowed

Daringly you smile
Purposely you advance
To what purpose?

Why me?

Silently I cry
Scream out in anguish
Body laden with weight
Pressed upon mine

Rancid breath
My cry's aloud or in my head?
Searing me apart
Why me?

Understand the impossible I cannot
No reasoning with his madness
Logic that has no pattern
A blend of unintelligible words

Blended with the best lies

CLAWS

A veil of love covers lying heart
I choose my darkened sanctuary

Do not test me

I will spit in your spiteful mouth
Bathe in your contempt

My nature is dark when defending
Light when embracing

You do not define me

Make of me what you wish
Wish it over and over again
Blow your candles and look upon a star
I will melt wax and cover those shiny stones with it
I will throw them deep in your heart and watch them sink

BEHIND CLOSED DOORS

I feel your gentle slap slowly caressing my face
That's what you see right?
When you drive the full force of your anger upon my open body
Love
When you whiplash my face with welts and colours
Care
When you stomp your truths and rights until you tire
Discipline
When you say I'm wrong
When you say I'm bad
When you say I deserve it

I hear my own song
Ringing in my ringing ear

I sing my own melody
Quietly from swollen lips

I see my own world
When I squint and wipe the blood

I will caress myself with time
I will kiss me with my own strength
I will push through the bruises

I'll unsheathe myself

VITA

KRONOS

Fluidity in motion
Carving its path through time
It commands
It does not reason
Slowly it quickly moves
Through lights in shadows
Through slanted air

It calls, it whispers, it shouts

Forever on the move
It hungers for your marrow

It waits, it watches, it knows

One tick tock into the next

BURNT

Surrounded by sea of fire
I burn myself
Charred steps trace traitorous journey
Cover each footprint in ashes
I breathe in deep fumes
They sting my throat
Singed tears scorch their path
Forever on
I feel everything
It burns and melts within
It freezes me into silence
Alone I trudge forward
Torched bones replace all that was
A final destination awaits

Will the flames cleanse or burn me to nothing?

THE STRUGGLE

You paint a picture of a thousand sorrows
Scars and welts hidden within
Silent laments in your laughter
Tap tap tap

Your foot does not obey you
Your leg
Your hand
All in unison
In their dormancy

Tap tap tap

I hear your sleeping foot
I hear your sigh and your groan
Dependence does not suit you

UNDERWATER

Submerged within my thoughts
I soak my heart in tears
They flood my being
unsoothe my soul
Eradicate what was

I froth
I freeze
I drown

In this reflected world
Immersed in my delusion
Cold
Shiver stirs

Leaves me undone

ENCHANTING NIGHT

Fluid night
Blender between worlds
Crisp and sweet you enter my soul

Magic night
My trusted loyal friend
Immortal you appear
Your potency surrounds
Yet cannot be touched
Clear yet dark
One yet all
As old as time
As deep and boundless as oceans

Unseen hand that caresses me to sleep while kissing me
    goodnight

BETWEEN RIGHT AND WRONG

Knock a hole through me
Under siege
Constant unrest follows constant retreat
Unmusical drum
Timeless in its incessant noise
Unwanted attention
"Please go away"
"Please let me be"
Pointing to past misdeeds
Past mistakes and sad goodbyes
It blows regret like windy rain
Can't escape their wetness
Wretchedly they mutate into dew drops
They cover me whole

Will I ever be dry?

FUNHOUSE

I cannot see the hidden
Fear freezes all senses
Ingrained
Where mirrors laugh
Grotesquely taunt
Reflecting shades of twisted glee
Mingling with shadow's black
Funhouse of exits leading to the start
Still I stand
Rooted
Trapped in place
Forever spinning

Forever dazed

NEW DAY

I awake from sweet limbo
Strip away
Doubts
Fears
Blurred insecurities
Stiff limbs fluid in motion
Propel me on
Clear water
Washes mud clean
While light glows with hope
Wrapping me unconditionally

I emerge

INSOMNIA

I lie here guarding your needs
Our views reflect absolute discord
Gradual rise of despair surpasses that of rage

Alone
My only solace coats the air
Soothing aching soul

For how long?

Melody flows slowly on
Embracing serene notes of warmth

Night on weary back awakens
Breathing cold air that breezes me in and out of
    consciousness
Incensed stifled tears awaken me
No control over them

While resting the restless night

THE GLINT IN YOUR EYE

Aimless wanderer wanders

Stands out for standing out
Attention un-sought but received
Eyes focus in general direction
Consciously ignores but subconsciously endures
Exploring is not the challenge

Being different is

Unable to dismiss looks and whispers
Eyes provoke back

HANTU AIR

Still walking water
Floats away from obscenity
Reflects in her shades of light
Drip your way into my soul
Shine like ripples from wondrous sky

Rush of water
Deadly strength
Infinity is announced
For granted it is taken
Boiling waves forth

Shake them down the river
Forever they rush on
They disturb the silence

Letting all unfold

LIKE CRYSTALS

Limpid darkness
Enclosed in stillness
Silently it strokes time forward
Moon radiates
Melting malice aside
A world of secrets revealed
Meshed with ardent lies
Luminously they pour
Cascading from the sky
Like crystals they fall

STORIES SHE TELLS

Her back turned

Speaks in tongues

Revels in her silent prayer

Listen carefully to her storytelling

She'll cry out of pasts, presents and futures

Dug out heart

Soaked in bloodied gold

Drips hope and despair alike

Yet she sits

Still

Straight

Back turned

Heart out

Sits still

With her silent prayer

MORNING AFTER

Whole body rocks with each empty retch

It trembles

Inwardly attempts to fight

All defences down

Tears streaming

A body full of nothing

Still it tries

It rocks

Contracting all limbs into a rigid mess

It cries out for release

EARTHLY SPLENDOR

The wind whispered and I received you
The earth groaned and I attached myself to vapours and
    lightnings
The night covers the world while I breathe in light
The rivers go wild
Sweaty brooks and dews
Muscular fields and mountains welcome me
The stars shine generously

While moon disappears beyond clouds

ALWAYS RIGHT

"Why won't you listen?"

"I do"

"If you did you wouldn't have this problem"

"It was an accident"

"Not listening was an accident?"

"No. Not that"

"Then what was?"

"Being wrong"

FIGHTER

Trapped in a prison of my own making
Barred from the choices I choose to let go
Narrowly I escape absolute darkness
Over and over again

Lights light the way forward
Shadows pursue
Confusion takes over
Chaos surrounds

What next?

Destruction of the ages

BLUE GRASS

What if the sky was green and the grass was blue?
To open up to the possibility that
anything is possible brings you
closer to being able to see your
world through unfiltered eyes

REBORN

Killing time that kills
Making presence known

Slowly I endure
Silently I ache
Surrounded by unwanted needs
To breathe
To think a burden
A forgotten chore
Distressed emotions flow
With them spine breaks inner core

Still I wake
I rise
Like ash
Cover all black
Softly I touch
I spread
I reach new heights
In search of light
I greed for it
Dig heels
I claw

I dust my all with shadowed hope
That day I'll be reborn

SHIFTER

Shifting in the night
Between moonbeams
Deathly pale I see you
Dreams untold
Lights reflecting from the now dark sky
In union they glisten
Force displayed is primal
Old and powerful
Velvety feel in night's mist
Surrounding
Binding me to you
Tears fall down from heavenly sky

Reflecting crying earth

GAZE LIKE MINE

We bleed into each other
Identities unknown

Averted eyes
See but don't see

I slip into my being
Slowly I rise

Muffled ears
Hear but don't hear

I take with me the meaning
Of mourning and light

Sealed lips
Speak but don't speak

I seek you out in fields
Of starry nights and highs

I wait
I hope
I pray

While I breathe

To meet a gaze like mine

UNTRUTHS

"So lying is bad?"

"Yes."

"What if it's to make you happy?"

"It's still bad."

"What if I can't help it?"

"You can always help it."

"How?"

"By telling the truth."

"What if the truth is a lie?"

"Then you keep telling that truth."

FEATHERS

I grow
Deep in the womb of time
I spread myself

I breathe
One tornado wrapped within a tsunami

I see
Infinity within my infinite song

I kill
One moist heart dripping on another

I burn
While I forever stamp on an expired wing

DEAD ASLEEP

They sleep the sleep of earth

Embraced by cycles
The forever green long gone

They wait

Earth's embrace
Smiles upon the fallen

Calling them home

ZEST OF HOPE

I need to keep looking at you
In these moments
Just you and I

I need to remind myself of that time
When I tripped through mixed emotions
When I rode a ride with no beginning and nearly no end
I stroke indentation on my skin

Slowly
Ink by ink

Life blinds us to the most valuable moments
How does that happen?
Periods in life that shape and make room for a new blurred one

Who decided it was time?
Was it even time?

I drew blood to remind me

If I close my eyes and focus I can almost feel it
Each sting
Each tingle
How I throbbed you into existence

ABOUT THE AUTHOR

HADINET TEKIE is a poet, artist, and creative visionary with a passion for language and a love of uplifting readers through her writing. As a dedicated wordsmith and the author of her debut poetry collection, *Stories She Tells*, Hadinet taps into the beauty and power of literature to share her reflections in a way that speaks to your soul. She hopes to immerse her readers in a profound spiritual and emotional journey, helping them rediscover the inquisitive individuals hiding deep within them and drawing out a source of imagination that they never knew they had.

Hadinet credits her writing to her diverse childhood, where she absorbed the rich details and experiences of countless different cultures and spheres of life. She's a natural-born dreamer, and she loves to empower the people around her to uncover their aspirations, express their emotions in new and authentic ways, and take the leap of faith to achieve their full potential. For more information about Hadinet and her work, visit her website at **www.dekove.me**

CREDITS

I would like to take this opportunity and thank the wonderful spirits that were manually involved behind the scenes to create my dream. They deserve recognition for their role in making my dream a reality. Thank you all!

Ellé Om	*Illustrator*
Karl	*Formatting and cover design*
Celia	*Proofreading*
Benjamin	*Project management*
Patrick	*CEO and owner of Publishing Push*
Linda and Sophie	*Sales*
Tarn	*Admin*

www.ingramcontent.com/pod-product-compliance
Lightning Source LLC
Chambersburg PA
CBHW041308110526
44590CB00028B/4294